THIS JOURNAL BELONGS TO:

_____

IF FOUND, RETURN TO:

_____
_____
_____

I created this journal based
on my experience as a
Certified Life Coach.

I currently specialize in working with teens and young adults so I know the importance of keeping things simple but effective.

Here's a tip I use with clients so they can be consistent with journaling:

Keep your journal where you charge your phone at night.
Write in the journal upon waking and before going to bed.

Enjoy!

All the best,

Aimee

Aimee Schlueter, CPC
Best in You Coaching
www.bestinyoucoaching.com

DATE: _____

MORNING

What I am grateful for today: _____

How I can be 1% better today: _____

Top priorities to accomplish today: First step to get started:

1. _____ ➔ 1. _____

2. _____ ➔ 2. _____

3. _____ ➔ 3. _____

Areas of self-care I want to improve on today and what action I will take:

_____

What I will do to give myself some fun and balance today after working hard:

_____

NIGHT

Self-Care Check-in:

- [ ] Ate Well
- [ ] Movement
- [ ] Drank Enough Water
- [ ] Sleep

How can I improve self-care tomorrow?

_____

What's something good that happened today?

_____

Looking back at my day, what am I grateful for?

_____

DATE: _____

MORNING

What I am grateful for today: _____

How I can be 1% better today: _____

Top priorities to accomplish today:			First step to get started:

1._____	➡	1._____
2._____	➡	2._____
3._____	➡	3._____

Areas of self-care I want to improve on today and what action I will take:
_____

What I will do to give myself some fun and balance today after working hard:
_____

NIGHT

Self-Care Check-in:

- [ ] Ate Well
- [ ] Drank Enough Water
- [ ] Movement
- [ ] Sleep

How can I improve self-care tomorrow?
_____

What's something good that happened today?
_____

Looking back at my day, what am I grateful for?
_____

DATE: _____

☀ MORNING

What I am grateful for today: _____

How I can be 1% better today: _____

Top priorities to accomplish today: First step to get started:

1._____ ➔ 1._____

2._____ ➔ 2._____

3._____ ➔ 3._____

Areas of self-care I want to improve on today and what action I will take:

_____

What I will do to give myself some fun and balance today after working hard:

_____

☾ NIGHT

Self-Care Check-in:

- [ ] Ate Well   - [ ] Movement
- [ ] Drank Enough Water - [ ] Sleep

How can I improve self-care tomorrow?

_____

What's something good that happened today?

_____

Looking back at my day, what am I grateful for?

_____

DATE: _____

MORNING

What I am grateful for today: _____

How I can be 1% better today: _____

Top priorities to accomplish today: First step to get started:

1._____ ➔ 1._____

2._____ ➔ 2._____

3._____ ➔ 3._____

Areas of self-care I want to improve on today and what action I will take:
_____

What I will do to give myself some fun and balance today after working hard:
_____

NIGHT

Self-Care Check-in:

- [ ] Ate Well
- [ ] Drank Enough Water
- [ ] Movement
- [ ] Sleep

How can I improve self-care tomorrow?
_____

What's something good that happened today?
_____

Looking back at my day, what am I grateful for?
_____

DATE: _____

☀ MORNING

What I am grateful for today: _____

How I can be 1% better today: _____

Top priorities to accomplish today: First step to get started:

1._____ ➡ 1._____

2._____ ➡ 2._____

3._____ ➡ 3._____

Areas of self-care I want to improve on today and what action I will take:

_____

What I will do to give myself some fun and balance today after working hard:

_____

☾ NIGHT

Self-Care Check-in:

- [ ] Ate Well
- [ ] Drank Enough Water
- [ ] Movement
- [ ] Sleep

How can I improve self-care tomorrow?

_____

What's something good that happened today?

_____

Looking back at my day, what am I grateful for?

_____

DATE: _____

MORNING

What I am grateful for today: _____

How I can be 1% better today: _____

Top priorities to accomplish today: First step to get started:

1. _____ ➡ 1. _____

2. _____ ➡ 2. _____

3. _____ ➡ 3. _____

Areas of self-care I want to improve on today and what action I will take:
_____

What I will do to give myself some fun and balance today after working hard:

_____

NIGHT

Self-Care Check-in:

☐ Ate Well   ☐ Movement
☐ Drank Enough Water ☐ Sleep

How can I improve self-care tomorrow?
_____

What's something good that happened today?
_____

Looking back at my day, what am I grateful for?
_____

DATE: _____

☀ MORNING

What I am grateful for today: _____

How I can be 1% better today: _____

Top priorities to accomplish today: First step to get started:

1._____ ➡ 1._____
2._____ ➡ 2._____
3._____ ➡ 3._____

Areas of self-care I want to improve on today and what action I will take:
_____

What I will do to give myself some fun and balance today after working hard:
_____

☾ NIGHT

Self-Care Check-in:

☐ Ate Well   ☐ Movement
☐ Drank Enough Water ☐ Sleep

How can I improve self-care tomorrow?
_____

What's something good that happened today?
_____

Looking back at my day, what am I grateful for?
_____

DATE: _____

MORNING

What I am grateful for today: _____

How I can be 1% better today: _____

Top priorities to accomplish today: First step to get started:

1. _____ → 1. _____
2. _____ → 2. _____
3. _____ → 3. _____

Areas of self-care I want to improve on today and what action I will take:
_____

What I will do to give myself some fun and balance today after working hard:
_____

NIGHT

Self-Care Check-in:

- [ ] Ate Well
- [ ] Drank Enough Water
- [ ] Movement
- [ ] Sleep

How can I improve self-care tomorrow?
_____

What's something good that happened today?
_____

Looking back at my day, what am I grateful for?
_____

DATE: _____

MORNING

What I am grateful for today: _____

How I can be 1% better today: _____

Top priorities to accomplish today: First step to get started:

1._____ → 1._____

2._____ → 2._____

3._____ → 3._____

Areas of self-care I want to improve on today and what action I will take:
_____

What I will do to give myself some fun and balance today after working hard:
_____

NIGHT

Self-Care Check-in:

☐ Ate Well	☐ Movement
☐ Drank Enough Water	☐ Sleep

How can I improve self-care tomorrow?
_____

What's something good that happened today?
_____

Looking back at my day, what am I grateful for?
_____

DATE: _____

MORNING

What I am grateful for today: _____

How I can be 1% better today: _____

Top priorities to accomplish today: First step to get started:

1._____ ➔ 1._____
2._____ ➔ 2._____
3._____ ➔ 3._____

Areas of self-care I want to improve on today and what action I will take:
_____

What I will do to give myself some fun and balance today after working hard:
_____

NIGHT

Self-Care Check-in:

- [ ] Ate Well   [ ] Movement
- [ ] Drank Enough Water   [ ] Sleep

How can I improve self-care tomorrow?
_____

What's something good that happened today?
_____

Looking back at my day, what am I grateful for?
_____

DATE: _____

☀ MORNING

What I am grateful for today: _____

How I can be 1% better today: _____

Top priorities to accomplish today: First step to get started:

1._____ ➡ 1._____

2._____ ➡ 2._____

3._____ ➡ 3._____

Areas of self-care I want to improve on today and what action I will take:
_____

What I will do to give myself some fun and balance today after working hard:
_____

☾ NIGHT

Self-Care Check-in:

☐ Ate Well   ☐ Movement
☐ Drank Enough Water   ☐ Sleep

How can I improve self-care tomorrow?
_____

What's something good that happened today?
_____

Looking back at my day, what am I grateful for?
_____

DATE: _____

MORNING

What I am grateful for today: _____

How I can be 1% better today: _____

Top priorities to accomplish today:			First step to get started:

1._____ ➡ 1._____

2._____ ➡ 2._____

3._____ ➡ 3._____

Areas of self-care I want to improve on today and what action I will take:
_____

What I will do to give myself some fun and balance today after working hard:
_____

NIGHT

Self-Care Check-in:

- ☐ Ate Well
- ☐ Drank Enough Water
- ☐ Movement
- ☐ Sleep

How can I improve self-care tomorrow?
_____

What's something good that happened today?
_____

Looking back at my day, what am I grateful for?
_____

DATE: _____

☀ MORNING

What I am grateful for today: _____

How I can be 1% better today: _____

Top priorities to accomplish today: First step to get started:

1._____ ⟶ 1._____

2._____ ⟶ 2._____

3._____ ⟶ 3._____

Areas of self-care I want to improve on today and what action I will take:
_____

What I will do to give myself some fun and balance today after working hard:
_____

☾ NIGHT

Self-Care Check-in:

- ☐ Ate Well   ☐ Movement
- ☐ Drank Enough Water ☐ Sleep

How can I improve self-care tomorrow?
_____

What's something good that happened today?
_____

Looking back at my day, what am I grateful for?
_____

DATE: _____

☀ MORNING

What I am grateful for today: _____

How I can be 1% better today: _____

Top priorities to accomplish today: First step to get started:

1._____ ➡ 1._____
2._____ ➡ 2._____
3._____ ➡ 3._____

Areas of self-care I want to improve on today and what action I will take:
_____

What I will do to give myself some fun and balance today after working hard:
_____

☾ NIGHT

Self-Care Check-in:

- [ ] Ate Well
- [ ] Drank Enough Water
- [ ] Movement
- [ ] Sleep

How can I improve self-care tomorrow?
_____

What's something good that happened today?
_____

Looking back at my day, what am I grateful for?
_____

DATE: _____

☀ MORNING

What I am grateful for today: _____

How I can be 1% better today: _____

Top priorities to accomplish today: First step to get started:

1. _____ ➔ 1. _____
2. _____ ➔ 2. _____
3. _____ ➔ 3. _____

Areas of self-care I want to improve on today and what action I will take:
_____

What I will do to give myself some fun and balance today after working hard:
_____

☾ NIGHT

Self-Care Check-in:

- [ ] Ate Well   - [ ] Movement
- [ ] Drank Enough Water - [ ] Sleep

How can I improve self-care tomorrow?
_____

What's something good that happened today?
_____

Looking back at my day, what am I grateful for?
_____

DATE: _____

☀ MORNING

What I am grateful for today: _____

How I can be 1% better today: _____

Top priorities to accomplish today: First step to get started:

1._____ ➔ 1._____
2._____ ➔ 2._____
3._____ ➔ 3._____

Areas of self-care I want to improve on today and what action I will take:
_____

What I will do to give myself some fun and balance today after working hard:
_____

☾ NIGHT

Self-Care Check-in:

☐ Ate Well   ☐ Movement
☐ Drank Enough Water   ☐ Sleep

How can I improve self-care tomorrow?
_____

What's something good that happened today?
_____

Looking back at my day, what am I grateful for?
_____

DATE: _____

☀ MORNING

What I am grateful for today: _____

How I can be 1% better today: _____

Top priorities to accomplish today: First step to get started:

1._____ ➔ 1._____

2._____ ➔ 2._____

3._____ ➔ 3._____

Areas of self-care I want to improve on today and what action I will take:
_____

What I will do to give myself some fun and balance today after working hard:
_____

☾ NIGHT

Self-Care Check-in:

- [ ] Ate Well   [ ] Movement
- [ ] Drank Enough Water [ ] Sleep

How can I improve self-care tomorrow?
_____

What's something good that happened today?
_____

Looking back at my day, what am I grateful for?
_____

DATE: _____

MORNING

What I am grateful for today: _____

How I can be 1% better today: _____

Top priorities to accomplish today: First step to get started:

1._____ ➡ 1._____

2._____ ➡ 2._____

3._____ ➡ 3._____

Areas of self-care I want to improve on today and what action I will take:
_____

What I will do to give myself some fun and balance today after working hard:
_____

NIGHT

Self-Care Check-in:

- [ ] Ate Well
- [ ] Drank Enough Water
- [ ] Movement
- [ ] Sleep

How can I improve self-care tomorrow?
_____

What's something good that happened today?
_____

Looking back at my day, what am I grateful for?
_____

DATE: _____

☀ MORNING

What I am grateful for today: _____

How I can be 1% better today: _____

Top priorities to accomplish today: First step to get started:

1._____ ➡ 1._____
2._____ ➡ 2._____
3._____ ➡ 3._____

Areas of self-care I want to improve on today and what action I will take:
_____

What I will do to give myself some fun and balance today after working hard:
_____

☾ NIGHT

Self-Care Check-in:

- [ ] Ate Well
- [ ] Drank Enough Water
- [ ] Movement
- [ ] Sleep

How can I improve self-care tomorrow?
_____

What's something good that happened today?
_____

Looking back at my day, what am I grateful for?
_____

DATE: _____

MORNING

What I am grateful for today: _____

How I can be 1% better today: _____

Top priorities to accomplish today: First step to get started:

1._____ ➔ 1._____
2._____ ➔ 2._____
3._____ ➔ 3._____

Areas of self-care I want to improve on today and what action I will take:
_____

What I will do to give myself some fun and balance today after working hard:
_____

NIGHT

Self-Care Check-in:

- ☐ Ate Well
- ☐ Drank Enough Water
- ☐ Movement
- ☐ Sleep

How can I improve self-care tomorrow?
_____

What's something good that happened today?
_____

Looking back at my day, what am I grateful for?
_____

DATE: _____

☀ MORNING

What I am grateful for today: _____

How I can be 1% better today: _____

Top priorities to accomplish today: First step to get started:

1._____   ➔   1._____
2._____   ➔   2._____
3._____   ➔   3._____

Areas of self-care I want to improve on today and what action I will take:
_____

What I will do to give myself some fun and balance today after working hard:
_____

☾ NIGHT

Self-Care Check-in:

☐ Ate Well   ☐ Movement
☐ Drank Enough Water ☐ Sleep

How can I improve self-care tomorrow?
_____

What's something good that happened today?
_____

Looking back at my day, what am I grateful for?
_____

DATE: _____

☀ MORNING

What I am grateful for today: _____

How I can be 1% better today: _____

Top priorities to accomplish today: First step to get started:

1._____ ➡ 1._____

2._____ ➡ 2._____

3._____ ➡ 3._____

Areas of self-care I want to improve on today and what action I will take:
_____

What I will do to give myself some fun and balance today after working hard:
_____

☾ NIGHT

Self-Care Check-in:

- ☐ Ate Well
- ☐ Drank Enough Water
- ☐ Movement
- ☐ Sleep

How can I improve self-care tomorrow?
_____

What's something good that happened today?
_____

Looking back at my day, what am I grateful for?
_____

DATE: _____

MORNING

What I am grateful for today: _____

How I can be 1% better today: _____

Top priorities to accomplish today: First step to get started:

1._____ ➔ 1._____
2._____ ➔ 2._____
3._____ ➔ 3._____

Areas of self-care I want to improve on today and what action I will take:
_____

What I will do to give myself some fun and balance today after working hard:
_____

NIGHT

Self-Care Check-in:

- [ ] Ate Well
- [ ] Drank Enough Water
- [ ] Movement
- [ ] Sleep

How can I improve self-care tomorrow?
_____

What's something good that happened today?
_____

Looking back at my day, what am I grateful for?
_____

DATE: _____

MORNING

What I am grateful for today: _____

How I can be 1% better today: _____

Top priorities to accomplish today:			First step to get started:

1._____	➡	1._____
2._____	➡	2._____
3._____	➡	3._____

Areas of self-care I want to improve on today and what action I will take:
_____

What I will do to give myself some fun and balance today after working hard:
_____

NIGHT

Self-Care Check-in:

☐ Ate Well   ☐ Movement
☐ Drank Enough Water   ☐ Sleep

How can I improve self-care tomorrow?
_____

What's something good that happened today?
_____

Looking back at my day, what am I grateful for?
_____

DATE: _____

MORNING

What I am grateful for today: _____

How I can be 1% better today: _____

Top priorities to accomplish today: First step to get started:

1. _____ → 1. _____
2. _____ → 2. _____
3. _____ → 3. _____

Areas of self-care I want to improve on today and what action I will take:
_____

What I will do to give myself some fun and balance today after working hard:
_____

NIGHT

Self-Care Check-in:

- [ ] Ate Well
- [ ] Drank Enough Water
- [ ] Movement
- [ ] Sleep

How can I improve self-care tomorrow?
_____

What's something good that happened today?
_____

Looking back at my day, what am I grateful for?
_____

DATE: _____

MORNING

What I am grateful for today: _____

How I can be 1% better today: _____

Top priorities to accomplish today: First step to get started:

1._____ ➡ 1._____

2._____ ➡ 2._____

3._____ ➡ 3._____

Areas of self-care I want to improve on today and what action I will take:
_____

What I will do to give myself some fun and balance today after working hard:
_____

NIGHT

Self-Care Check-in:

- ☐ Ate Well
- ☐ Drank Enough Water
- ☐ Movement
- ☐ Sleep

How can I improve self-care tomorrow?
_____

What's something good that happened today?
_____

Looking back at my day, what am I grateful for?
_____

DATE: _____

☀ MORNING

What I am grateful for today: _____

How I can be 1% better today: _____

Top priorities to accomplish today: First step to get started:

1._____ ➡ 1._____

2._____ ➡ 2._____

3._____ ➡ 3._____

Areas of self-care I want to improve on today and what action I will take:
_____

What I will do to give myself some fun and balance today after working hard:
_____

🌙 NIGHT

Self-Care Check-in:

☐ Ate Well   ☐ Movement
☐ Drank Enough Water   ☐ Sleep

How can I improve self-care tomorrow?
_____

What's something good that happened today?
_____

Looking back at my day, what am I grateful for?
_____

DATE: _____

MORNING

What I am grateful for today: _____

How I can be 1% better today: _____

Top priorities to accomplish today: First step to get started:

1._____   ➡   1._____
2._____   ➡   2._____
3._____   ➡   3._____

Areas of self-care I want to improve on today and what action I will take:
_____

What I will do to give myself some fun and balance today after working hard:
_____

NIGHT

Self-Care Check-in:

- [ ] Ate Well
- [ ] Drank Enough Water
- [ ] Movement
- [ ] Sleep

How can I improve self-care tomorrow?
_____

What's something good that happened today?
_____

Looking back at my day, what am I grateful for?
_____

DATE: _____

☀ MORNING

What I am grateful for today: _____

How I can be 1% better today: _____

Top priorities to accomplish today: First step to get started:

1._____ ➤ 1._____

2._____ ➤ 2._____

3._____ ➤ 3._____

Areas of self-care I want to improve on today and what action I will take:
_____

What I will do to give myself some fun and balance today after working hard:
_____

☾ NIGHT

Self-Care Check-in:

☐ Ate Well   ☐ Movement
☐ Drank Enough Water   ☐ Sleep

How can I improve self-care tomorrow?
_____

What's something good that happened today?
_____

Looking back at my day, what am I grateful for?
_____

DATE: _____

☀ MORNING

What I am grateful for today: _____

How I can be 1% better today: _____

Top priorities to accomplish today: First step to get started:

1._____ ➡ 1._____

2._____ ➡ 2._____

3._____ ➡ 3._____

Areas of self-care I want to improve on today and what action I will take:
_____

What I will do to give myself some fun and balance today after working hard:
_____

☾ NIGHT

Self-Care Check-in:

- [ ] Ate Well
- [ ] Drank Enough Water
- [ ] Movement
- [ ] Sleep

How can I improve self-care tomorrow?
_____

What's something good that happened today?
_____

Looking back at my day, what am I grateful for?
_____

DATE: _____

☀ MORNING

What I am grateful for today: _____

How I can be 1% better today: _____

Top priorities to accomplish today: First step to get started:

1._____ ➔ 1._____
2._____ ➔ 2._____
3._____ ➔ 3._____

Areas of self-care I want to improve on today and what action I will take:
_____

What I will do to give myself some fun and balance today after working hard:
_____

☾ NIGHT

Self-Care Check-in:

☐ Ate Well	☐ Movement
☐ Drank Enough Water	☐ Sleep

How can I improve self-care tomorrow?
_____

What's something good that happened today?
_____

Looking back at my day, what am I grateful for?
_____

DATE: _____

MORNING

What I am grateful for today: _____

How I can be 1% better today: _____

Top priorities to accomplish today: First step to get started:

1. _____ ➡ 1. _____
2. _____ ➡ 2. _____
3. _____ ➡ 3. _____

Areas of self-care I want to improve on today and what action I will take:
_____

What I will do to give myself some fun and balance today after working hard:
_____

NIGHT

Self-Care Check-in:

- [ ] Ate Well   - [ ] Movement
- [ ] Drank Enough Water - [ ] Sleep

How can I improve self-care tomorrow?
_____

What's something good that happened today?
_____

Looking back at my day, what am I grateful for?
_____

DATE: _____

MORNING

What I am grateful for today: _____

How I can be 1% better today: _____

Top priorities to accomplish today: First step to get started:

1. _____ → 1. _____
2. _____ → 2. _____
3. _____ → 3. _____

Areas of self-care I want to improve on today and what action I will take:
_____

What I will do to give myself some fun and balance today after working hard:
_____

NIGHT

Self-Care Check-in:

- [ ] Ate Well
- [ ] Drank Enough Water
- [ ] Movement
- [ ] Sleep

How can I improve self-care tomorrow?
_____

What's something good that happened today?
_____

Looking back at my day, what am I grateful for?
_____

DATE: _____

MORNING

What I am grateful for today: _____

How I can be 1% better today: _____

Top priorities to accomplish today:　　　　First step to get started:

1._____ ➡ 1._____

2._____ ➡ 2._____

3._____ ➡ 3._____

Areas of self-care I want to improve on today and what action I will take:
_____

What I will do to give myself some fun and balance today after working hard:
_____

NIGHT

Self-Care Check-in:

- [ ] Ate Well
- [ ] Drank Enough Water
- [ ] Movement
- [ ] Sleep

How can I improve self-care tomorrow?
_____

What's something good that happened today?
_____

Looking back at my day, what am I grateful for?
_____

DATE: _____

☀ MORNING

What I am grateful for today: _____

How I can be 1% better today: _____

Top priorities to accomplish today: First step to get started:

1. _____ ➔ 1. _____
2. _____ ➔ 2. _____
3. _____ ➔ 3. _____

Areas of self-care I want to improve on today and what action I will take:
_____

What I will do to give myself some fun and balance today after working hard:
_____

☾ NIGHT

Self-Care Check-in:

☐ Ate Well   ☐ Movement
☐ Drank Enough Water ☐ Sleep

How can I improve self-care tomorrow?
_____

What's something good that happened today?
_____

Looking back at my day, what am I grateful for?
_____

DATE: _____

MORNING

What I am grateful for today: _____

How I can be 1% better today: _____

Top priorities to accomplish today: First step to get started:

1._____ ➔ 1._____
2._____ ➔ 2._____
3._____ ➔ 3._____

Areas of self-care I want to improve on today and what action I will take:
_____

What I will do to give myself some fun and balance today after working hard:
_____

NIGHT

Self-Care Check-in:

- [ ] Ate Well
- [ ] Drank Enough Water
- [ ] Movement
- [ ] Sleep

How can I improve self-care tomorrow?
_____

What's something good that happened today?
_____

Looking back at my day, what am I grateful for?
_____

DATE: _____

☀ MORNING

What I am grateful for today: _____

How I can be 1% better today: _____

Top priorities to accomplish today: First step to get started:

1. _____ ➔ 1. _____
2. _____ ➔ 2. _____
3. _____ ➔ 3. _____

Areas of self-care I want to improve on today and what action I will take:
_____

What I will do to give myself some fun and balance today after working hard:
_____

☾ NIGHT

Self-Care Check-in:

☐ Ate Well	☐ Movement
☐ Drank Enough Water	☐ Sleep

How can I improve self-care tomorrow?
_____

What's something good that happened today?
_____

Looking back at my day, what am I grateful for?
_____

DATE: _____

MORNING

What I am grateful for today: _____

How I can be 1% better today: _____

Top priorities to accomplish today: First step to get started:

1._____ ➡ 1._____

2._____ ➡ 2._____

3._____ ➡ 3._____

Areas of self-care I want to improve on today and what action I will take:
_____

What I will do to give myself some fun and balance today after working hard:
_____

NIGHT

Self-Care Check-in:

- [ ] Ate Well
- [ ] Drank Enough Water
- [ ] Movement
- [ ] Sleep

How can I improve self-care tomorrow?
_____

What's something good that happened today?
_____

Looking back at my day, what am I grateful for?
_____

DATE: _____

☀ MORNING

What I am grateful for today: _____

How I can be 1% better today: _____

Top priorities to accomplish today: First step to get started:

1. _____ ➔ 1. _____

2. _____ ➔ 2. _____

3. _____ ➔ 3. _____

Areas of self-care I want to improve on today and what action I will take:
_____

What I will do to give myself some fun and balance today after working hard:
_____

☾ NIGHT

Self-Care Check-in:

- [ ] Ate Well   [ ] Movement
- [ ] Drank Enough Water   [ ] Sleep

How can I improve self-care tomorrow?
_____

What's something good that happened today?
_____

Looking back at my day, what am I grateful for?
_____

DATE: _____

MORNING

What I am grateful for today: _____

How I can be 1% better today: _____

Top priorities to accomplish today: First step to get started:

1. _____ → 1. _____
2. _____ → 2. _____
3. _____ → 3. _____

Areas of self-care I want to improve on today and what action I will take:
_____

What I will do to give myself some fun and ba ance today after working hard:
_____

NIGHT

Self-Care Check-in:

- [ ] Ate Well   - [ ] Movement
- [ ] Drank Enough Water - [ ] Sleep

How can I improve self-care tomorrow?
_____

What's something good that happened today?
_____

Looking back at my day, what am I grateful for?
_____

DATE: _____

☀ MORNING

What I am grateful for today: _____

How I can be 1% better today: _____

Top priorities to accomplish today: First step to get started:

1._____ ➔ 1._____

2._____ ➔ 2._____

3._____ ➔ 3._____

Areas of self-care I want to improve on today and what action I will take:
_____

What I will do to give myself some fun and balance today after working hard:
_____

☾ NIGHT

Self-Care Check-in:

- ☐ Ate Well
- ☐ Drank Enough Water
- ☐ Movement
- ☐ Sleep

How can I improve self-care tomorrow?
_____

What's something good that happened today?
_____

Looking back at my day, what am I grateful for?
_____

DATE: _____

MORNING

What I am grateful for today: _____

How I can be 1% better today: _____

Top priorities to accomplish today: First step to get started:

1._____ ➔ 1._____

2._____ ➔ 2._____

3._____ ➔ 3._____

Areas of self-care I want to improve on today and what action I will take:
_____

What I will do to give myself some fun and balance today after working hard:
_____

NIGHT

Self-Care Check-in:

- ☐ Ate Well
- ☐ Drank Enough Water
- ☐ Movement
- ☐ Sleep

How can I improve self-care tomorrow?
_____

What's something good that happened today?
_____

Looking back at my day, what am I grateful for?
_____

DATE: _____

☀ MORNING

What I am grateful for today: _____

How I can be 1% better today: _____

Top priorities to accomplish today: First step to get started:

1. _____ ➔ 1. _____

2. _____ ➔ 2. _____

3. _____ ➔ 3. _____

Areas of self-care I want to improve on today and what action I will take:
_____

What I will do to give myself some fun and balance today after working hard:
_____

☾ NIGHT

Self-Care Check-in:

- [ ] Ate Well
- [ ] Drank Enough Water
- [ ] Movement
- [ ] Sleep

How can I improve self-care tomorrow?
_____

What's something good that happened today?
_____

Looking back at my day, what am I grateful for?
_____

DATE: _____

☀ MORNING

What I am grateful for today: _____

How I can be 1% better today: _____

Top priorities to accomplish today: First step to get started:

1. _____ ➡ 1. _____

2. _____ ➡ 2. _____

3. _____ ➡ 3. _____

Areas of self-care I want to improve on today and what action I will take:
_____

What I will do to give myself some fun and balance today after working hard:
_____

☾ NIGHT

Self-Care Check-in:

- ☐ Ate Well
- ☐ Drank Enough Water
- ☐ Movement
- ☐ Sleep

How can I improve self-care tomorrow?
_____

What's something good that happened today?
_____

Looking back at my day, what am I grateful for?
_____

DATE: _____

☀ MORNING

What I am grateful for today: _____

How I can be 1% better today: _____

Top priorities to accomplish today: First step to get started:

1._____ ➡ 1._____

2._____ ➡ 2._____

3._____ ➡ 3._____

Areas of self-care I want to improve on today and what action I will take:
_____

What I will do to give myself some fun and balance today after working hard:
_____

🌙 NIGHT

Self-Care Check-in:

☐ Ate Well   ☐ Movement
☐ Drank Enough Water ☐ Sleep

How can I improve self-care tomorrow?
_____

What's something good that happened today?
_____

Looking back at my day, what am I grateful for?
_____

DATE: _____

MORNING

What I am grateful for today: _____

How I can be 1% better today: _____

Top priorities to accomplish today: First step to get started:

1._____ ➔ 1._____
2._____ ➔ 2._____
3._____ ➔ 3._____

Areas of self-care I want to improve on today and what action I will take:
_____

What I will do to give myself some fun and balance today after working hard:
_____

NIGHT

Self-Care Check-in:

- [ ] Ate Well
- [ ] Drank Enough Water
- [ ] Movement
- [ ] Sleep

How can I improve self-care tomorrow?
_____

What's something good that happened today?
_____

Looking back at my day, what am I grateful for?
_____

DATE: _____

☀ MORNING

What I am grateful for today: _____

How I can be 1% better today: _____

Top priorities to accomplish today: First step to get started:

1._____   ➡   1._____

2._____   ➡   2._____

3._____   ➡   3._____

Areas of self-care I want to improve on today and what action I will take:
_____

What I will do to give myself some fun and balance today after working hard:
_____

🌙 NIGHT

Self-Care Check-in:

☐ Ate Well   ☐ Movement
☐ Drank Enough Water ☐ Sleep

How can I improve self-care tomorrow?
_____

What's something good that happened today?
_____

Looking back at my day, what am I grateful for?
_____

DATE: _____

MORNING

What I am grateful for today: _____

How I can be 1% better today: _____

Top priorities to accomplish today: First step to get started:

1._____ ➔ 1._____

2._____ ➔ 2._____

3._____ ➔ 3._____

Areas of self-care I want to improve on today and what action I will take:

_____

What I will do to give myself some fun and balance today after working hard:

_____

NIGHT

Self-Care Check-in:

- [ ] Ate Well
- [ ] Drank Enough Water
- [ ] Movement
- [ ] Sleep

How can I improve self-care tomorrow?

_____

What's something good that happened today?

_____

Looking back at my day, what am I grateful for?

_____

DATE: _____

MORNING

What I am grateful for today: _____

How I can be 1% better today: _____

Top priorities to accomplish today: First step to get started:

1._____   ➔   1._____
2._____   ➔   2._____
3._____   ➔   3._____

Areas of self-care I want to improve on today and what action I will take:
_____

What I will do to give myself some fun and balance today after working hard:
_____

NIGHT

Self-Care Check-in:

☐ Ate Well   ☐ Movement
☐ Drank Enough Water   ☐ Sleep

How can I improve self-care tomorrow?
_____

What's something good that happened today?
_____

Looking back at my day, what am I grateful for?
_____

DATE: _____

MORNING

What I am grateful for today: _____

How I can be 1% better today: _____

Top priorities to accomplish today: First step to get started:

1._____ ➡ 1._____

2._____ ➡ 2._____

3._____ ➡ 3._____

Areas of self-care I want to improve on today and what action I will take:
_____

What I will do to give myself some fun and balance today after working hard:
_____

NIGHT

Self-Care Check-in:

- [ ] Ate Well
- [ ] Drank Enough Water
- [ ] Movement
- [ ] Sleep

How can I improve self-care tomorrow?
_____

What's something good that happened today?
_____

Looking back at my day, what am I grateful for?
_____

DATE: _____

☀ MORNING

What I am grateful for today: _____

How I can be 1% better today: _____

Top priorities to accomplish today: First step to get started:

1._____ ➔ 1._____

2._____ ➔ 2._____

3._____ ➔ 3._____

Areas of self-care I want to improve on today and what action I will take:
_____

What I will do to give myself some fun and balance today after working hard:
_____

☾ NIGHT

Self-Care Check-in:

- [ ] Ate Well   - [ ] Movement
- [ ] Drank Enough Water - [ ] Sleep

How can I improve self-care tomorrow?
_____

What's something good that happened today?
_____

Looking back at my day, what am I grateful for?
_____

DATE: _____

MORNING

What I am grateful for today: _____

How I can be 1% better today: _____

Top priorities to accomplish today: First step to get started:

1._____ ➡ 1._____

2._____ ➡ 2._____

3._____ ➡ 3._____

Areas of self-care I want to improve on today and what action I will take:
_____

What I will do to give myself some fun and balance today after working hard:
_____

NIGHT

Self-Care Check-in:

☐ Ate Well	☐ Movement
☐ Drank Enough Water	☐ Sleep

How can I improve self-care tomorrow?
_____

What's something good that happened today?
_____

Looking back at my day, what am I grateful for?
_____

DATE: _____

☀ MORNING

What I am grateful for today: _____

How I can be 1% better today: _____

Top priorities to accomplish today: First step to get started:

1._____ ➡ 1._____

2._____ ➡ 2._____

3._____ ➡ 3._____

Areas of self-care I want to improve on today and what action I will take:
_____

What I will do to give myself some fun and balance today after working hard:
_____

☾ NIGHT

Self-Care Check-in:

- [ ] Ate Well   - [ ] Movement
- [ ] Drank Enough Water - [ ] Sleep

How can I improve self-care tomorrow?
_____

What's something good that happened today?
_____

Looking back at my day, what am I grateful for?
_____

DATE: _____

MORNING

What I am grateful for today: _____

How I can be 1% better today: _____

Top priorities to accomplish today: First step to get started:

1._____ ➡ 1._____

2._____ ➡ 2._____

3._____ ➡ 3._____

Areas of self-care I want to improve on today and what action I will take:
_____

What I will do to give myself some fun and balance today after working hard:
_____

NIGHT

Self-Care Check-in:

- [ ] Ate Well
- [ ] Drank Enough Water
- [ ] Movement
- [ ] Sleep

How can I improve self-care tomorrow?
_____

What's something good that happened today?
_____

Looking back at my day, what am I grateful for?
_____

DATE: _____

☀ MORNING

What I am grateful for today: _____

How I can be 1% better today: _____

Top priorities to accomplish today: First step to get started:

1._____ ➡ 1._____
2._____ ➡ 2._____
3._____ ➡ 3._____

Areas of self-care I want to improve on today and what action I will take:
_____

What I will do to give myself some fun and balance today after working hard:
_____

🌙 NIGHT

Self-Care Check-in:

- ☐ Ate Well
- ☐ Drank Enough Water
- ☐ Movement
- ☐ Sleep

How can I improve self-care tomorrow?
_____

What's something good that happened today?
_____

Looking back at my day, what am I grateful for?
_____

DATE: _____

☀ MORNING

What I am grateful for today: _____

How I can be 1% better today: _____

Top priorities to accomplish today: First step to get started:

1._____ ➡ 1._____

2._____ ➡ 2._____

3._____ ➡ 3._____

Areas of self-care I want to improve on today and what action I will take:
_____

What I will do to give myself some fun and balance today after working hard:
_____

☾ NIGHT

Self-Care Check-in:

- ☐ Ate Well
- ☐ Drank Enough Water
- ☐ Movement
- ☐ Sleep

How can I improve self-care tomorrow?
_____

What's something good that happened today?
_____

Looking back at my day, what am I grateful for?
_____

DATE: _____

☀ MORNING

What I am grateful for today: _____

How I can be 1% better today: _____

Top priorities to accomplish today: First step to get started:

1._____ ➔ 1._____

2._____ ➔ 2._____

3._____ ➔ 3._____

Areas of self-care I want to improve on today and what action I will take:
_____

What I will do to give myself some fun and balance today after working hard:
_____

☾ NIGHT

Self-Care Check-in:

☐ Ate Well	☐ Movement
☐ Drank Enough Water	☐ Sleep

How can I improve self-care tomorrow?
_____

What's something good that happened today?
_____

Looking back at my day, what am I grateful for?
_____

DATE: _____

MORNING

What I am grateful for today: _____

How I can be 1% better today: _____

Top priorities to accomplish today: First step to get started:

1._____ ➡ 1._____
2._____ ➡ 2._____
3._____ ➡ 3._____

Areas of self-care I want to improve on today and what action I will take:
_____

What I will do to give myself some fun and balance today after working hard:
_____

NIGHT

Self-Care Check-in:

- [ ] Ate Well
- [ ] Drank Enough Water
- [ ] Movement
- [ ] Sleep

How can I improve self-care tomorrow?
_____

What's something good that happened today?
_____

Looking back at my day, what am I grateful for?
_____

DATE: _____

☀ MORNING

What I am grateful for today: _____

How I can be 1% better today: _____

Top priorities to accomplish today: First step to get started:

1._____ ➡ 1._____

2._____ ➡ 2._____

3._____ ➡ 3._____

Areas of self-care I want to improve on today and what action I will take:
_____

What I will do to give myself some fun and balance today after working hard:
_____

🌙 NIGHT

Self-Care Check-in:

- [ ] Ate Well   - [ ] Movement
- [ ] Drank Enough Water - [ ] Sleep

How can I improve self-care tomorrow?
_____

What's something good that happened today?
_____

Looking back at my day, what am I grateful for?
_____

DATE: _____

☀ MORNING

What I am grateful for today: _____

How I can be 1% better today: _____

Top priorities to accomplish today: First step to get started:

1. _____ ➔ 1. _____
2. _____ ➔ 2. _____
3. _____ ➔ 3. _____

Areas of self-care I want to improve on today and what action I will take:
_____

What I will do to give myself some fun and balance today after working hard:
_____

☾ NIGHT

Self-Care Check-in:

☐ Ate Well	☐ Movement
☐ Drank Enough Water	☐ Sleep

How can I improve self-care tomorrow?
_____

What's something good that happened today?
_____

Looking back at my day, what am I grateful for?
_____

DATE: _____

☀ MORNING

What I am grateful for today: _____

How I can be 1% better today: _____

Top priorities to accomplish today: First step to get started:

1._____ ➜ 1._____
2._____ ➜ 2._____
3._____ ➜ 3._____

Areas of self-care I want to improve on today and what action I will take:
_____

What I will do to give myself some fun and balance today after working hard:
_____

☾ NIGHT

Self-Care Check-in:

- [ ] Ate Well
- [ ] Drank Enough Water
- [ ] Movement
- [ ] Sleep

How can I improve self-care tomorrow?
_____

What's something good that happened today?
_____

Looking back at my day, what am I grateful for?
_____

DATE: _____

MORNING

What I am grateful for today: _____

How I can be 1% better today: _____

Top priorities to accomplish today: First step to get started:

1._____   ➔   1._____

2._____   ➔   2._____

3._____   ➔   3._____

Areas of self-care I want to improve on today and what action I will take:
_____

What I will do to give myself some fun and balance today after working hard:
_____

NIGHT

Self-Care Check-in:

☐ Ate Well	☐ Movement
☐ Drank Enough Water	☐ Sleep

How can I improve self-care tomorrow?
_____

What's something good that happened today?
_____

Looking back at my day, what am I grateful for?
_____

DATE: _____

MORNING

What I am grateful for today: _____

How I can be 1% better today: _____

Top priorities to accomplish today: First step to get started:

1. _____ → 1. _____
2. _____ → 2. _____
3. _____ → 3. _____

Areas of self-care I want to improve on today and what action I will take:
_____

What I will do to give myself some fun and balance today after working hard:
_____

NIGHT

Self-Care Check-in:

- [ ] Ate Well
- [ ] Drank Enough Water
- [ ] Movement
- [ ] Sleep

How can I improve self-care tomorrow?
_____

What's something good that happened today?
_____

Looking back at my day, what am I grateful for?
_____

DATE: _____

MORNING

What I am grateful for today: _____

How I can be 1% better today: _____

Top priorities to accomplish today: First step to get started:

1._____ ➡ 1._____

2._____ ➡ 2._____

3._____ ➡ 3._____

Areas of self-care I want to improve on today and what action I will take:
_____

What I will do to give myself some fun and balance today after working hard:
_____

NIGHT

Self-Care Check-in:

- ☐ Ate Well
- ☐ Drank Enough Water
- ☐ Movement
- ☐ Sleep

How can I improve self-care tomorrow?
_____

What's something good that happened today?
_____

Looking back at my day, what am I grateful for?
_____

DATE: _____

MORNING

What I am grateful for today: _____

How I can be 1% better today: _____

Top priorities to accomplish today: First step to get started:

1. _____ ➤ 1. _____

2. _____ ➤ 2. _____

3. _____ ➤ 3. _____

Areas of self-care I want to improve on today and what action I will take:

_____

What I will do to give myself some fun and balance today after working hard:

_____

NIGHT

Self-Care Check-in:

- [ ] Ate Well
- [ ] Drank Enough Water
- [ ] Movement
- [ ] Sleep

How can I improve self-care tomorrow?

_____

What's something good that happened today?

_____

Looking back at my day, what am I grateful for?

_____

DATE: _____

MORNING

What I am grateful for today: _____

How I can be 1% better today: _____

Top priorities to accomplish today: First step to get started:

1._____   ➔   1._____

2._____   ➔   2._____

3._____   ➔   3._____

Areas of self-care I want to improve on today and what action I will take:
_____

What I will do to give myself some fun and balance today after working hard:
_____

NIGHT

Self-Care Check-in:

☐ Ate Well	☐ Movement
☐ Drank Enough Water	☐ Sleep

How can I improve self-care tomorrow?
_____

What's something good that happened today?
_____

Looking back at my day, what am I grateful for?
_____

DATE: _____

MORNING

What I am grateful for today: _____

How I can be 1% better today: _____

Top priorities to accomplish today: First step to get started:

1._____   →   1._____

2._____   →   2._____

3._____   →   3._____

Areas of self-care I want to improve on today and what action I will take:
_____

What I will do to give myself some fun and balance today after working hard:
_____

NIGHT

Self-Care Check-in:

- [ ] Ate Well   - [ ] Movement
- [ ] Drank Enough Water   - [ ] Sleep

How can I improve self-care tomorrow?
_____

What's something good that happened today?
_____

Looking back at my day, what am I grateful for?
_____

DATE: _____

MORNING

What I am grateful for today: _____

How I can be 1% better today: _____

Top priorities to accomplish today: First step to get started:

1._____ ➔ 1._____

2._____ ➔ 2._____

3._____ ➔ 3._____

Areas of self-care I want to improve on today and what action I will take:
_____

What I will do to give myself some fun and balance today after working hard:
_____

NIGHT

Self-Care Check-in:

- [ ] Ate Well   - [ ] Movement
- [ ] Drank Enough Water - [ ] Sleep

How can I improve self-care tomorrow?
_____

What's something good that happened today?
_____

Looking back at my day, what am I grateful for?
_____

DATE: _____

MORNING

What I am grateful for today: _____

How I can be 1% better today: _____

Top priorities to accomplish today: First step to get started:

1. _____   ➡   1. _____
2. _____   ➡   2. _____
3. _____   ➡   3. _____

Areas of self-care I want to improve on today and what action I will take:
_____

What I will do to give myself some fun and balance today after working hard:
_____

NIGHT

Self-Care Check-in:

- [ ] Ate Well
- [ ] Drank Enough Water
- [ ] Movement
- [ ] Sleep

How can I improve self-care tomorrow?
_____

What's something good that happened today?
_____

Looking back at my day, what am I grateful for?
_____

DATE: _____

MORNING

What I am grateful for today: _____

How I can be 1% better today: _____

Top priorities to accomplish today: First step to get started:

1._____ → 1._____

2._____ → 2._____

3._____ → 3._____

Areas of self-care I want to improve on today and what action I will take:
_____

What I will do to give myself some fun and balance today after working hard:
_____

NIGHT

Self-Care Check-in:

- [ ] Ate Well
- [ ] Drank Enough Water
- [ ] Movement
- [ ] Sleep

How can I improve self-care tomorrow?
_____

What's something good that happened today?
_____

Looking back at my day, what am I grateful for?
_____

DATE: _____

☀ MORNING

What I am grateful for today: _____

How I can be 1% better today: _____

Top priorities to accomplish today: First step to get started:

1._____ ➤ 1._____
2._____ ➤ 2._____
3._____ ➤ 3._____

Areas of self-care I want to improve on today and what action I will take:
_____

What I will do to give myself some fun and balance today after working hard:
_____

☾ NIGHT

Self-Care Check-in:

☐ Ate Well   ☐ Movement
☐ Drank Enough Water ☐ Sleep

How can I improve self-care tomorrow?
_____

What's something good that happened today?
_____

Looking back at my day, what am I grateful for?
_____

DATE: _____

☀ MORNING

What I am grateful for today: _____

How I can be 1% better today: _____

Top priorities to accomplish today: First step to get started:

1._____ ➔ 1._____

2._____ ➔ 2._____

3._____ ➔ 3._____

Areas of self-care I want to improve on today and what action I will take:
_____

What I will do to give myself some fun and balance today after working hard:
_____

☾ NIGHT

Self-Care Check-in:

- [ ] Ate Well
- [ ] Drank Enough Water
- [ ] Movement
- [ ] Sleep

How can I improve self-care tomorrow?
_____

What's something good that happened today?
_____

Looking back at my day, what am I grateful for?
_____

DATE: _____

MORNING

What I am grateful for today: _____

How I can be 1% better today: _____

Top priorities to accomplish today: First step to get started:

1. _____ → 1. _____
2. _____ → 2. _____
3. _____ → 3. _____

Areas of self-care I want to improve on today and what action I will take:
_____

What I will do to give myself some fun and balance today after working hard:
_____

NIGHT

Self-Care Check-in:

- [ ] Ate Well
- [ ] Drank Enough Water
- [ ] Movement
- [ ] Sleep

How can I improve self-care tomorrow?
_____

What's something good that happened today?
_____

Looking back at my day, what am I grateful for?
_____

DATE: _____

☀ MORNING

What I am grateful for today: _____

How I can be 1% better today: _____

Top priorities to accomplish today: First step to get started:

1._____ ➡ 1._____

2._____ ➡ 2._____

3._____ ➡ 3._____

Areas of self-care I want to improve on today and what action I will take:
_____

What I will do to give myself some fun and balance today after working hard:
_____

☾ NIGHT

Self-Care Check-in:

- [ ] Ate Well
- [ ] Drank Enough Water
- [ ] Movement
- [ ] Sleep

How can I improve self-care tomorrow?
_____

What's something good that happened today?
_____

Looking back at my day, what am I grateful for?
_____

DATE: _____

MORNING

What I am grateful for today: _____

How I can be 1% better today: _____

Top priorities to accomplish today: First step to get started:

1._____ ➡ 1._____

2._____ ➡ 2._____

3._____ ➡ 3._____

Areas of self-care I want to improve on today and what action I will take:
_____

What I will do to give myself some fun and balance today after working hard:
_____

NIGHT

Self-Care Check-in:

☐ Ate Well   ☐ Movement
☐ Drank Enough Water ☐ Sleep

How can I improve self-care tomorrow?
_____

What's something good that happened today?
_____

Looking back at my day, what am I grateful for?
_____

DATE: _____

MORNING

What I am grateful for today: _____

How I can be 1% better today: _____

Top priorities to accomplish today: First step to get started:

1._____ ➔ 1._____

2._____ ➔ 2._____

3._____ ➔ 3._____

Areas of self-care I want to improve on today and what action I will take:
_____

What I will do to give myself some fun and balance today after working hard:
_____

NIGHT

Self-Care Check-in:

☐ Ate Well   ☐ Movement
☐ Drank Enough Water   ☐ Sleep

How can I improve self-care tomorrow?
_____

What's something good that happened today?
_____

Looking back at my day, what am I grateful for?
_____

DATE: _____

MORNING

What I am grateful for today: _____

How I can be 1% better today: _____

Top priorities to accomplish today: First step to get started:

1. _____ ➡ 1. _____
2. _____ ➡ 2. _____
3. _____ ➡ 3. _____

Areas of self-care I want to improve on today and what action I will take:

_____

What I will do to give myself some fun and balance today after working hard:

_____

NIGHT

Self-Care Check-in:

- [ ] Ate Well
- [ ] Drank Enough Water
- [ ] Movement
- [ ] Sleep

How can I improve self-care tomorrow?

_____

What's something good that happened today?

_____

Looking back at my day, what am I grateful for?

_____

DATE: _____

☀ MORNING

What I am grateful for today: _____

How I can be 1% better today: _____

Top priorities to accomplish today: First step to get started:

1._____ ➜ 1._____
2._____ ➜ 2._____
3._____ ➜ 3._____

Areas of self-care I want to improve on today and what action I will take:
_____

What I will do to give myself some fun and balance today after working hard:
_____

☾ NIGHT

Self-Care Check-in:

- ☐ Ate Well   ☐ Movement
- ☐ Drank Enough Water   ☐ Sleep

How can I improve self-care tomorrow?
_____

What's something good that happened today?
_____

Looking back at my day, what am I grateful for?
_____

DATE: _____

MORNING

What I am grateful for today: _____

How I can be 1% better today: _____

Top priorities to accomplish today:			First step to get started:

1. _____ ➡ 1. _____

2. _____ ➡ 2. _____

3. _____ ➡ 3. _____

Areas of self-care I want to improve on today and what action I will take:

_____

What I will do to give myself some fun and balance today after working hard:

_____

NIGHT

Self-Care Check-in:

☐ Ate Well   ☐ Movement
☐ Drank Enough Water ☐ Sleep

How can I improve self-care tomorrow?

_____

What's something good that happened today?

_____

Looking back at my day, what am I grateful for?

_____

DATE: _____

MORNING

What I am grateful for today: _____

How I can be 1% better today: _____

Top priorities to accomplish today: First step to get started:

1._____ ➡ 1._____

2._____ ➡ 2._____

3._____ ➡ 3._____

Areas of self-care I want to improve on today and what action I will take:

_____

What I will do to give myself some fun and balance today after working hard:

_____

NIGHT

Self-Care Check-in:

- ☐ Ate Well   ☐ Movement
- ☐ Drank Enough Water ☐ Sleep

How can I improve self-care tomorrow?

_____

What's something good that happened today?

_____

Looking back at my day, what am I grateful for?

_____

DATE: _____

MORNING

What I am grateful for today: _____

How I can be 1% better today: _____

Top priorities to accomplish today: First step to get started:

1._____ ➔ 1._____
2._____ ➔ 2._____
3._____ ➔ 3._____

Areas of self-care I want to improve on today and what action I will take:
_____

What I will do to give myself some fun and balance today after working hard:
_____

NIGHT

Self-Care Check-in:

☐ Ate Well   ☐ Movement
☐ Drank Enough Water   ☐ Sleep

How can I improve self-care tomorrow?
_____

What's something good that happened today?
_____

Looking back at my day, what am I grateful for?
_____

DATE: _____

MORNING

What I am grateful for today: _____

How I can be 1% better today: _____

Top priorities to accomplish today: First step to get started:

1._____ ➡ 1._____

2._____ ➡ 2._____

3._____ ➡ 3._____

Areas of self-care I want to improve on today and what action I will take:

_____

What I will do to give myself some fun and balance today after working hard:

_____

NIGHT

Self-Care Check-in:

- [ ] Ate Well
- [ ] Drank Enough Water
- [ ] Movement
- [ ] Sleep

How can I improve self-care tomorrow?

_____

What's something good that happened today?

_____

Looking back at my day, what am I grateful for?

_____

DATE: _____

MORNING

What I am grateful for today: _____

How I can be 1% better today: _____

Top priorities to accomplish today: First step to get started:

1. _____   ➔   1. _____

2. _____   ➔   2. _____

3. _____   ➔   3. _____

Areas of self-care I want to improve on today and what action I will take:
_____

What I will do to give myself some fun and balance today after working hard:
_____

NIGHT

Self-Care Check-in:

- ☐ Ate Well
- ☐ Drank Enough Water
- ☐ Movement
- ☐ Sleep

How can I improve self-care tomorrow?
_____

What's something good that happened today?
_____

Looking back at my day, what am I grateful for?
_____

DATE: _____

MORNING

What I am grateful for today: _____

How I can be 1% better today: _____

Top priorities to accomplish today: First step to get started:

1. _____ ➡ 1. _____

2. _____ ➡ 2. _____

3. _____ ➡ 3. _____

Areas of self-care I want to improve on today and what action I will take:

_____

What I will do to give myself some fun and balance today after working hard:

_____

NIGHT

Self-Care Check-in:

- [ ] Ate Well
- [ ] Drank Enough Water
- [ ] Movement
- [ ] Sleep

How can I improve self-care tomorrow?

_____

What's something good that happened today?

_____

Looking back at my day, what am I grateful for?

_____

DATE: _____

☀ MORNING

What I am grateful for today: _____

How I can be 1% better today: _____

Top priorities to accomplish today: First step to get started:

1._____   ➡   1._____

2._____   ➡   2._____

3._____   ➡   3._____

Areas of self-care I want to improve on today and what action I will take:
_____

What I will do to give myself some fun and balance today after working hard:
_____

☾ NIGHT

Self-Care Check-in:

☐ Ate Well   ☐ Movement
☐ Drank Enough Water   ☐ Sleep

How can I improve self-care tomorrow?
_____

What's something good that happened today?
_____

Looking back at my day, what am I grateful for?
_____

DATE: _____

MORNING

What I am grateful for today: _____

How I can be 1% better today: _____

Top priorities to accomplish today: First step to get started:

1._____ ➡ 1._____
2._____ ➡ 2._____
3._____ ➡ 3._____

Areas of self-care I want to improve on today and what action I will take:
_____

What I will do to give myself some fun and balance today after working hard:
_____

NIGHT

Self-Care Check-in:

- [ ] Ate Well   - [ ] Movement
- [ ] Drank Enough Water - [ ] Sleep

How can I improve self-care tomorrow?
_____

What's something good that happened today?
_____

Looking back at my day, what am I grateful for?
_____

DATE: _____

MORNING

What I am grateful for today: _____

How I can be 1% better today: _____

Top priorities to accomplish today: First step to get started:

1. _____ ➡ 1. _____
2. _____ ➡ 2. _____
3. _____ ➡ 3. _____

Areas of self-care I want to improve on today and what action I will take:

_____

What I will do to give myself some fun and balance today after working hard:

_____

NIGHT

Self-Care Check-in:

- [ ] Ate Well
- [ ] Drank Enough Water
- [ ] Movement
- [ ] Sleep

How can I improve self-care tomorrow?

_____

What's something good that happened today?

_____

Looking back at my day, what am I grateful for?

_____

DATE: _____

MORNING

What I am grateful for today: _____

How I can be 1% better today: _____

Top priorities to accomplish today: First step to get started:

1._____ ➔ 1._____
2._____ ➔ 2._____
3._____ ➔ 3._____

Areas of self-care I want to improve on today and what action I will take:

_____

What I will do to give myself some fun and balance today after working hard:

_____

NIGHT

Self-Care Check-in:

- [ ] Ate Well
- [ ] Drank Enough Water
- [ ] Movement
- [ ] Sleep

How can I improve self-care tomorrow?

_____

What's something good that happened today?

_____

Looking back at my day, what am I grateful for?

_____

DATE: _____

MORNING

What I am grateful for today: _____

How I can be 1% better today: _____

Top priorities to accomplish today: First step to get started:

1. _____ ➡ 1. _____

2. _____ ➡ 2. _____

3. _____ ➡ 3. _____

Areas of self-care I want to improve on today and what action I will take:
_____

What I will do to give myself some fun and balance today after working hard:
_____

NIGHT

Self-Care Check-in:

- [ ] Ate Well
- [ ] Drank Enough Water
- [ ] Movement
- [ ] Sleep

How can I improve self-care tomorrow?
_____

What's something good that happened today?
_____

Looking back at my day, what am I grateful for?
_____

DATE: _____

☀ MORNING

What I am grateful for today: _____

How I can be 1% better today: _____

Top priorities to accomplish today: First step to get started:

1._____ ➡ 1._____

2._____ ➡ 2._____

3._____ ➡ 3._____

Areas of self-care I want to improve on today and what action I will take:
_____

What I will do to give myself some fun and balance today after working hard:
_____

☾ NIGHT

Self-Care Check-in:

- [ ] Ate Well
- [ ] Drank Enough Water
- [ ] Movement
- [ ] Sleep

How can I improve self-care tomorrow?
_____

What's something good that happened today?
_____

Looking back at my day, what am I grateful for?
_____

DATE: _____

☀ MORNING

What I am grateful for today: _____

How I can be 1% better today: _____

Top priorities to accomplish today: First step to get started:

1. _____ ➜ 1. _____
2. _____ ➜ 2. _____
3. _____ ➜ 3. _____

Areas of self-care I want to improve on today and what action I will take:
_____

What I will do to give myself some fun and balance today after working hard:
_____

☾ NIGHT

Self-Care Check-in:

- [ ] Ate Well   - [ ] Movement
- [ ] Drank Enough Water - [ ] Sleep

How can I improve self-care tomorrow?
_____

What's something good that happened today?
_____

Looking back at my day, what am I grateful for?
_____

DATE: _____

MORNING

What I am grateful for today: _____

How I can be 1% better today: _____

Top priorities to accomplish today: First step to get started:

1._____ ➔ 1._____

2._____ ➔ 2._____

3._____ ➔ 3._____

Areas of self-care I want to improve on today and what action I will take:

_____

What I will do to give myself some fun and balance today after working hard:

_____

NIGHT

Self-Care Check-in:

- [ ] Ate Well
- [ ] Drank Enough Water
- [ ] Movement
- [ ] Sleep

How can I improve self-care tomorrow?

_____

What's something good that happened today?

_____

Looking back at my day, what am I grateful for?

_____

Made in the USA
Columbia, SC
17 March 2025